JUEL ANDERSEN'S

CAROB PRIMER

BOOKS BY JUEL ANDERSEN:

THE TOFU COOKBOOK   (WITH CATHY BAUER)

JUEL ANDERSEN'S TOFU KITCHEN

TOFU PRIMER

TOFU FANTASIES

BY JUEL ANDERSEN & ROBIN CLUTE

TEMPEH PRIMER

JUEL ANDERSEN'S
CAROB PRIMER

A BEGINNER'S BOOK OF CAROB COOKERY

ROBIN CLUTE

JUEL ANDERSEN

WITH   **SIGRID ANDERSEN**

Illustrations also from Mother Goose's Nursery Rhymes, McLoughlin Brothers, 1930 and Mother Goose's Nursery Rhymes, Cupples & Leon Co., 1930

Illustrations by permission of Dover Publications, Inc., New York, N.Y. from: *Food and Drink:* a Pictorial Archive from 19th Century Sources, edited by Jim Harter, 1979; and *Calligraphy:* by Johann George Schwanander, 1958.

Book Design and Lettering by Sigrid Andersen

ISBN 0-916870-60-X

Published by
CREATIVE ARTS COMMUNICATIONS
833 Bancroft Way, Berkeley, California 94701

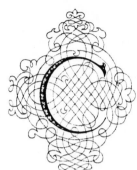

CONTENTS

I NTRODUCING

CAROB

CAROB IS A FLAVORING. IT IS ALSO A NUTRITIOUS FOOD. IT COMES IN MANY FORMS, BUT IT HAS BECOME MOST FAMILIAR AS SOMETHING AKIN TO CHOCOLATE.

CHOCOLATE IS ALSO A FLAVORING. BUT, IT IS ONLY MARGINALLY NUTRITIOUS. IN FACT, IT IS POSITIVELY BAD FOR MANY PEOPLE. IT IS HIGH IN FAT, THEREFORE ALSO HIGH IN CALORIES. IT CONTAINS CAFFEINE AND THEOBROMINE, BOTH STIMULANTS, AND OXALIC ACID, WHICH PREVENTS CALCIUM ABSORPTION AND BINDS IRON SO IT CAN NOT BE USED BY THE BODY.

BUT COMPARISONS WITH CHOCOLATE ARE WIDE SPREAD AND PEOPLE THINK OF CAROB AS CHOCOLATE-LIKE. IT MAY LOOK THE SAME, BE THE SAME COLOR, AND BE USED IN SIMILAR WAYS, BUT IT JUST DOES NOT TASTE THE SAME, NOR SHOULD IT BE EXPECTED TO.

CAROB IS NATURALLY SWEET, INDEED, IT CAN BE USED AS A SWEETENER ITSELF. CHOCOLATE IS SO BITTER THAT HUGE AMOUNTS OF SUGAR MUST BE ADDED TO IT TO MAKE IT PALATABLE.

CAROB IS HIGH IN CALCIUM, LOW IN SODIUM, HIGH IN POTASSIUM AND IRON, RICH IN PECTIN AND IS A GOOD SOURCE OF VITAMIN A AND THE B VITAMINS.

INDEED, IT IS CALLED "ST. JOHN'S BREAD". THE BIBLE* TELLS US THAT THE BAPTIST EXISTED IN THE WILDERNESS ON "LOCUSTS AND HONEY." THE LOCUST REFERRED TO IS NOT THE INSECT, AS MANY HAVE THOUGHT, BUT THE POD OF THE LOCUST TREE, OR CAROB TREE (CERATONIA SILIQUA). IT IS NATIVE TO THE MEDITERRANEAN COUNTRIES. MENTION OF CAROB HAS BEEN FOUND IN GREEK AND ROMAN WRITINGS, AND SEEDS AND PODS WERE FOUND IN ANCIENT EGYPTIAN TOMBS.

Carob.
a, leaves; b, bloom; c, fruit.

CAROB POWDER IS MADE BY GRINDING AND ROASTING CAROB PODS. THE SEEDS IN THE PODS ARE NOT PROCESSED INTO CAROB POWDER, BUT ARE USED TO MAKE THE FOOD, GUM TRAGACANTH. THIS GUM IS WIDELY USED IN PROCESSED FOODS AS A THICKENER AND STABILIZER. THE NEXT TIME YOU EAT FLAVORED YOGURT OR OR ICE CREAM, READ THE INGREDIENTS LIST. CHANCES ARE IT WILL INCLUDE CAROB OR LOCUST BEAN GUM.

* MATTHEW 3:4, MARK 1:6

2

CAROB CHIPS AND CANDY COATINGS ARE MADE FROM CAROB POWDER MIXED WITH OIL, POWDERED MILK, AND SUGAR. THESE CAROB PRODUCTS TASTE THE MOST LIKE CHOCOLATE BECAUSE OF THEIR HIGH FAT AND SUGAR CONTENT. UNSWEETENED CAROB CHIPS ARE AVAILABLE IN NATURAL FOOD STORES. THEY RELY ON CAROB'S NATURAL SWEETNESS FOR THEIR FLAVOR. WHILE THEY DO NOT TASTE LIKE CHOCOLATE, THEY ADD A DELICIOUS RICHNESS AND FLAVOR TO BAKED FOODS, AND THEY MELT BEAUTIFULLY.

CAROB POWDER IS USUALLY SOLD ALREADY ROASTED. THIS GIVES IT A DARK, RICH COLOR AND IMPROVES THE FLAVOR. IF THE CAROB POWDER YOU PURCHASE IS NOT ROASTED YOU CAN DO IT YOURSELF. DRY ROAST THE CAROB POWDER ON AN UNGREASED BAKING SHEET IN A LOW (150°) OVEN UNTIL IT IS RICH BROWN AND SMELLS DELICIOUS. YOU CAN ALSO ROAST CAROB POWDER IN AN UNOILED, HEAVY SKILLET OVER LOW HEAT. STIR FREQUENTLY UNTIL BROWNED, BUT NOT BURNT!

BAKED GOODS MADE WITH CAROB POWDER TEND TO BROWN FAST. WATCH THEM CAREFULLY, AND/OR LOWER OVEN TEMPERATURE BY 25° FOR THE LAST 10 TO 15 MINUTES OF BAKING. IT IS A GOOD IDEA TO SIFT CAROB POWDER WITH THE OTHER DRY INGREDIENTS TO MAKE SURE IT IS WELL MIXED.

CAROB POWDER WILL LUMP WHEN ADDED TO LIQUIDS. USE A BLENDER TO MIX IT WELL OR ADD LIQUID SLOWLY TO THE CAROB, STIRRING CONSTANTLY WITH A WIRE WHISK. CAROB MIXES MORE EASILY WITH WARM LIQUIDS. IT NEVER COMPLETELY DISSOLVES, HOWEVER. WHEN MAKING CAROB DRINKS, STIR BEFORE SERVING, AND EXPECT TO SEE A LAYER OF CAROB "SEDIMENT" AT THE BOTTOM OF YOUR CUP.

CAROB ADDS SUBTLE SWEETNESS AND BEAUTIFUL COLOR TO RECIPES NOT NORMALLY ASSOCIATED WITH CHOCOLATE. TRY IT IN BRAN MUFFINS (BRAN-APPLE MUFFINS, PAGE 36), GINGERBREAD, (GINGERBREAD, PAGE 28), OR CREPES (CAROB CREPE DESSERT, PAGE 25) FOR A NEW TASTE TREAT. CAROB ALSO TASTES DELICIOUS IN TRADITIONAL CHOCOLATE GOODIES SUCH AS CUPCAKES, COOKIES, MILK SHAKES, ICE CREAM TOPPINGS, AND BROWNIES. TRY CAROB IN MANY WAYS; ENJOY ITS FLAVOR, COLOR AND AROMA. YOU WILL BE TREATING NOT ONLY YOUR TASTE BUDS, BUT YOUR BODY AS WELL!

USING CAROB INSTEAD OF CHOCOLATE

CAROB ADDS A PLEASANTLY SWEET TASTE, DELICIOUS AROMA, AND BEAUTIFUL DARK COLOR WHEREVER IT IS USED. AND CAROB'S NUTRITIONAL BENEFITS DEFINITELY MAKE IT WORTH GETTING TO KNOW.

♥ SUBSTITUTE EQUAL AMOUNTS OF CAROB POWDER FOR UNSWEETENED COCOA. REMEMBER THAT CAROB IS HALF AS SWEET AS SUGAR AND REDUCE SWEETENER CALLED FOR BY AT LEAST 1/4.

4

♥ TO REPLACE 1 SQUARE (1 OUNCE) OF UNSWEETENED BAKING CHOCOLATE, STIR TOGETHER 3 TBSP. CAROB POWDER, 1 TBSP. WATER AND ONE OR TWO DROPS OF VANILLA EXTRACT. THIS WILL NOT HAVE THE OIL CONTENT OF CHOCOLATE; YOU MAY WANT TO ADD AN EXTRA TBSP. OF FAT FOR EVERY OUNCE OF CHOCOLATE THE RECIPE CALLS FOR.

♥ WHEN SUBSTITUTING FOR UNSWEETENED CHOCOLATE, REMEMBER THAT CAROB IS SWEET, NOT BITTER. ADDING 1 TO 2 TEASPOONS OF INSTANT COFFEE POWDER TO THE RECIPE WILL MAKE FOR A MORE "CHOCOLATY" (BITTER) TASTE.

♥ USE SWEETENED OR UNSWEETENED CAROB CHIPS INSTEAD OF CHOCOLATE CHIPS IN ANY COOKIE RECIPE ~ THEY ARE INTERCHANGEABLE. IF THE RECIPE CALLS FOR SEMI-SWEET CHOCOLATE CHIPS, UNSWEETENED CAROB CHIPS WILL TASTE BETTER.

♥ FOR MELTED MILK CHOCOLATE OR CHOCOLATE CHIPS, SUBSTITUTE SWEETENED CAROB CHIPS AND ADD 2 TABLESPOONS POWDERED MILK TO THE DRY INGREDIENTS FOR EVERY 4 OUNCES OF CHOCOLATE USED.

♥ USE A DOUBLE BOILER TO MELT EITHER SWEETENED OR UNSWEETENED CAROB CHIPS. THE WATER MUST NOT TOUCH THE TOP, AND BE KEPT AT JUST BELOW A BOIL. PUT THE THE CAROB CHIPS IN THE TOP PAN AND STIR UNTIL THEY ARE MELTED. MELTED CAROB CHIPS CAN BE USED FOR DIPPING, AS A FROSTING, OR THE BASIS OF MANY DELICIOUS CONFECTIONS LIKE THE RAISIN-NUT CANDIES ON PAGE 12, OR OAT BROWNIES ON PAGE 13.

 **NOTES**

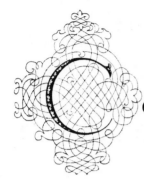

COOKIES, BROWNIES, & CANDIES

The Dancing Crocodile

A merry musician wandered once
On the banks of the river Nile;
Imagine his fright, there hove in sight
A monstrous Crocodile.
His teeth were long, his jaws were strong,
His mouth was horribly wide;
And he grinned a grin, "Dear Sir, come in,
There's plenty of room inside!"

ICE BOX COOKIES

MAKES 4 DOZEN

```
1 3/4  CUPS  WHOLE WHEAT PASTRY FLOUR
1/4    CUP   POWDERED MILK
1/4    CUP   CAROB POWDER
1/2    TSP.  BAKING POWDER
1/4    TSP.  SALT
3/4    CUP   BUTTER OR MARGARINE
1      CUP   BROWN SUGAR
1            EGG
1      TSP.  VANILLA
1      TBSP. MILK OR BUTTERMILK
1/2    CUP   CAROB CHIPS AND/OR NUTS
```

SIFT FLOUR, POWDERED MILK, CAROB POWDER, BAKING POWDER, AND SALT TOGETHER AND SET ASIDE. CREAM THE BUTTER AND BROWN SUGAR AND ADD THE EGG, VANILLA, AND MILK. BEAT UNTIL FLUFFY.

COARSELY CHOP THE CAROB CHIPS AND/OR NUTS AND STIR INTO FLOUR MIXTURE. MIX FLOUR INTO THE BUTTER-HONEY MIXTURE BY HAND OR IN A FOOD PROCESSOR UNTIL DOUGH IS SMOOTH. IT WILL BE VERY THICK. FORM DOUGH INTO ROLLS, EACH ABOUT TWO INCHES THICK. WRAP IN WAXED PAPER OR PLASTIC WRAP AND CHILL FOR AT LEAST LEAST TWO HOURS. (DOUGH CAN BE FROZEN TOO.)

HEAT OVEN TO 325°. SLICE DOUGH 1/4 INCH THICK. PLACE COOKIES ON A GREASED COOKIE SHEET. BAKE 12 TO 15 MINUTES UNTIL FIRM. COOL ON RACKS.

COCON-OAT COOKIES

MAKES 4 DOZEN

<u>PRE~HEAT OVEN TO 350°</u>

2 CUPS ROLLED OATS
3/4 CUP HONEY
1 EGG
1 TSP. VANILLA
1/2 CUP MELTED BUTTER OR MARGARINE
2 TBSP. MILK
3/4 TSP. SALT
1/2 TSP. BAKING SODA
4 TBSP. CAROB POWDER, SIFTED
1 1/2 CUPS UNSWEETENED, GRATED COCONUT

PUT OATS IN A BLENDER 1 CUP AT A TIME AND PROCESS A FEW MINUTES UNTIL GROUND INTO A COARSE FLOUR. SET ASIDE. BEAT TOGETHER THE HONEY, EGG, VANILLA, MELTED BUTTER, AND MILK. MIX THE CAROB POWDER, SALT, AND SODA IN A CUP AND ADD TO THE HONEY MIXTURE. ADD THE OAT FLOUR AND BEAT WELL, THEN STIR IN COCONUT. DROP BY ROUNDED TEASPOONFULS ONTO A GREASED COOKIE SHEET. FLATTEN EACH COOKIE WITH A WET FORK. BAKE AT 350° FOR 12 TO 15 MINUTES. LET COOL ON BAKING SHEET FOR 5 MINUTES BEFORE REMOVING. STORE COOKIES AIR TIGHT IN A METAL OR PLASTIC CONTAINER.

RUM BALLS

MAKES 40 1" BALLS

A SPECIAL UNCOOKED TREAT!

1 CUP SWEET CRUMBS: GRAHAM CRACKER, OLD COOKIE, DRY CAKE, ETC.
1/2 CUP CAROB CHIPS
1/4 CUP CAROB POWDER
1/2 CUP NUT MEATS: NOT PEANUTS
2 TBSP. CORN STARCH
1/8 TSP. SALT (OPTIONAL)
2 TSP. VANILLA
1/4 CUP RUM
2 TBSP. HONEY
1 TO 2 TBSP. SOFT BUTTER OR MARGARINE
1/2 CUP CHOPPED NUTS

COMBINE THE CRUMBS, CAROB CHIPS, CAROB POWDER, NUTS, CORN STARCH, AND SALT IN A FOOD PROCESSOR OR BLENDER AND PROCESS UNTIL VERY FINE. ADD VANILLA, RUM AND HONEY AND BLEND WELL. ADD 1 TABLESPOON BUTTER TO THE MIXTURE AND BLEND UNTIL IT FORMS A BALL. IF IT DOES NOT HOLD TOGETHER WELL, ADD MORE SHORTENING.

ROLL INTO 1 INCH BALLS AND ROLL IN CHOPPED NUTS. CHILL BEFORE SERVING. THESE CANDIES RIPEN WITH AGE.

PEANUT BUTTER FUDGE

MAKES ABOUT 24 SQUARES

1/2 CUP HONEY
1 CUP NATURAL PEANUT BUTTER
1/3 CUP CAROB POWDER
1/2 CUP CHOPPED NUTS
ABOUT 1/2 CUP POWDERED MILK
INSTANT OR NON-INSTANT

WARM HONEY IN A SAUCEPAN, THEN REMOVE FROM HEAT AND ADD THE PEANUT BUTTER. MIX WELL, THEN STIR IN THE CAROB POWDER. ADD NUTS, THEN STIR OR KNEAD IN ENOUGH POWDERED MILK TO MAKE THE FUDGE FIRM BUT NOT CRUMBLY. THE AMOUNT USED DEPENDS ON THE OIL CONTENT OF THE PEANUT BUTTER.

PRESS THE FUDGE INTO A BREAD PAN, PRESSING IT INTO AN EVEN LAYER ABOUT 1 INCH THICK. CUT INTO SQUARES AND REFRIGERATE TO KEEP IT FROM GETTING SOFT.

RAISIN-NUT CANDIES

MAKES 12 TO 20

1/2 CUP CAROB CHIPS
1/4 CUP RAISINS
1/4 CUP COARSELY
CHOPPED NUTS

MELT THE CAROB CHIPS IN THE TOP OF A DOUBLE BOILER, MAKING SURE THAT THE WATER DOES NOT TOUCH THE PAN; HEAT FROM STEAM WILL MELT THE CAROB CHIPS, OTHERWISE THE TEXTURE WILL BE GRAINY. STIR UNTIL SMOOTH; ADD THE RAISINS AND NUTS AND MIX UNTIL THEY ARE COATED. SPOON ONTO A GREASED PLATE AND REFRIGERATE UNTIL SET AND STORE IN A CLOSED CONTAINER.

SO EASY IT'S EMBARRASSING...

OAT BROWNIES

MAKES 16 TO 20 BROWNIES

AN EXTRA SPECIAL TREAT!

PRE-HEAT OVEN TO 350°

```
3/4  CUP   CAROB CHIPS
            (UNSWEETENED IS BEST)
1/4  CUP   BUTTER
2    EGGS
1/2  CUP   BROWN SUGAR
1    CUP   ROLLED OATS
1/2  TSP.  BAKING POWDER
1/2  TSP.  SALT
1    TSP.  VANILLA
1    CUP   CHOPPED NUTS
```

MELT THE CAROB CHIPS AND BUTTER IN A DOUBLE BOILER OVER HOT BUT NOT BOILING WATER; COOL SLIGHTLY BEFORE USING. MEANWHILE, COMBINE SUGAR, AND OATS IN A FOOD PROCESSOR OR BLENDER AND PROCESS UNTIL OATS ARE CHOPPED FINE. SET ASIDE. THEN BEAT EGGS UNTIL LIGHT AND FLUFFY. ADD OAT MIXTURE, BAKING POWDER, SALT, AND VANILLA AND PROCESS BRIEFLY.

STIR OAT MIXTURE INTO MELTED CAROB MIXTURE ALONG WITH NUTS. SPOON INTO A GREASED 8 INCH SQUARE PAN. BAKE AT 350° FOR 30 MINUTES, OR UNTIL FIRM IN CENTER. COOL ON A RACK AND THE THEN CUT INTO SQUARES.

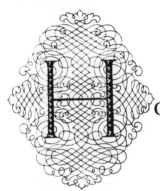

HONEY BROWNIES

FILLS AN 8 INCH SQUARE PAN

<u>PRE-HEAT OVEN TO 350°</u>

1/2 CUP BUTTER OR MARGARINE
2/3 CUP HONEY
2 EGGS
1/2 TSP. SALT
1 TSP. VANILLA
2/3 CUP WHOLE WHEAT PASTRY FLOUR
1/3 CUP CAROB POWDER
1 TSP. BAKING POWDER
3 TBSP. POWDERED MILK
1 CUP CHOPPED NUTS

CREAM BUTTER AND HONEY TOGETHER. ADD EGGS, SALT, AND VANILLA AND BEAT UNTIL FLUFFY.

SIFT THE FLOUR, CAROB POWDER, BAKING POWDER, AND POWDERED MILK TOGETHER. BLEND INTO BUTTER-HONEY MIXTURE, THEN STIR IN THE CHOPPED NUTS. TURN INTO A GREASED 8 INCH SQUARE PAN. BAKE AT 350° FOR 30 TO 35 MINUTES, OR UNTIL CAKE TESTS DONE. AND EDGES ARE PULLING AWAY FROM THE SIDES OF THE PAN. COOL ON A RACK AND CUT INTO SQUARES.

CRANOLA TREATS

```
2/3  CUP  CAROB  CHIPS
 1   TBSP.  HONEY
 2   TBSP.  MARGARINE  OR  BUTTER
1 1/2  CUPS  GRANOLA
1/2  CUP  COARSELY  CHOPPED  NUTS
```

COMBINE THE CAROB CHIPS, HONEY, AND BUTTER IN THE TOP OF A DOUBLE BOILER AND MELT OVER MEDIUM HEAT, STIRRING CONSTANTLY. DO NOT LET THE WATER TOUCH THE BOTTOM OF THE DOUBLE BOILER TOP, AS THE CAROB WILL NOT MELT PROPERLY. WHEN MELTED AND MIXED, STIR IN THE GRANOLA AND NUTS. DROP BY SPOONFULS INTO SMALL PAPER CUPS AND REFRIGERATOR UNTIL SET.

AROB DOTS

MAKES 4 DOZEN COOKIES

```
1   CUP  BUTTER  OR  MARGARINE
1   CUP  BROWN  SUGAR
2   EGGS
1/2  CUP  YOGURT  OR  BUTTERMILK
1   TSP.  VANILLA
2   CUPS  UNBLEACHED  WHITE
              FLOUR
1/3  CUP  CAROB  POWDER
1   TSP.  BAKING  POWDER
1/2  TSP.  SALT
1/4  CUP  BROWN  SUGAR
1   TBSP.  CAROB  POWDER
2   TBSP.  CAROB  CHIPS
```

CREAM BUTTER AND SUGAR TOGETHER.
BEAT IN EGGS, THEN YOGURT AND VANILLA UNTIL
LIGHT AND FLUFFY.   SIFT TOGETHER: FLOUR, CAROB
POWDER, BAKING POWDER, AND SALT.   BLEND
FLOUR MIXTURE AND BUTTER MIXTURE UNTIL A
SOFT DOUGH FORMS.   CHILL   SEVERAL   HOURS.

MIX   1/4 CUP BROWN SUGAR AND
1 TBSP. CAROB POWDER AND SPREAD
OUT ON A PLATE.   DROP ROUNDED
TEASPOONSFUL OF DOUGH ON THE
PLATE AND COAT WELL WITH THE
CAROB - SUGAR MIXTURE AND
THEN ROLL INTO BALLS.
PLACE   ON   GREASED
BAKING SHEETS, ABOUT 2 INCHES APART.   PRESS
1 OR 2 CAROB CHIPS INTO THE CENTER OF EACH
BALL, FLATTENING IT SLIGHTLY.   BAKE AT
ONCE AT 375° FOR 12 TO 15 MINUTES.   LET
SIT ON COOKIE SHEET 2 MINUTES BEFORE
REMOVING TO A RACK TO COOL.

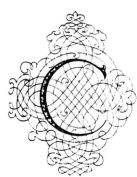

CAROB CHIPPERS

1/2	CUP	SOFTENED BUTTER OR MARGARINE
3/4	CUP	HONEY
2		EGGS
1	TSP.	VANILLA
2	CUPS	WHOLE WHEAT PASTRY FLOUR
1/4	CUP	SOY FLOUR
1/2	TSP.	SALT (OPTIONAL)
2	TSP.	BAKING POWDER
1	CUP	CHOPPED NUTS
1	CUP	CAROB CHIPS

CREAM BUTTER AND HONEY. ADD EGGS AND VANILLA AND BEAT UNTIL FLUFFY. SIFT TOGETHER FLOUR, SOY FLOUR, SALT, AND BAKING POWDER AND ADD TO THE TO THE BUTTER MIXTURE, MIXING WELL. STIR IN THE NUTS AND CAROB CHIPS. CHILL DOUGH AT LEAST 1 HOUR. DROP BY SPOONSFUL ONTO OILED COOKIE SHEETS. BAKE AT 350° FOR 10 TO 12 MINUTES.

DELICIOUS !

 **NOTES**

SAUCES, SHAKES, & CREPES

The merry musician shook with fear,
He shivered from hat to shoe,
"You are ever so kind, but if you don't mind
I'd rather not lunch with you."

"Try it at least,"
said the scaly beast,
With a broad malicious smile;
"You'll see in a trice
how quiet and nice,
It is to eat by the Nile."

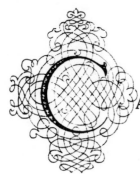

AROB SYRUP

MAKES 2 1/2 CUPS

3 TBSP. BUTTER OR MARGARINE
2 TBSP. WHOLE WHEAT FLOUR
3 TBSP. CAROB POWDER
2 CUPS MILK
1/4 CUP BROWN SUGAR OR HONEY (OR TO TASTE)
1/2 CUP POWDERED MILK
1 TSP. VANILLA

MELT BUTTER OVER LOW HEAT. SIFT FLOUR AND CAROB POWDER TOGETHER. STIR INTO MELTED BUTTER. VERY SLOWLY, ADD THE MILK, STIRRING CONSTANTLY TO MAKE A SMOOTH SAUCE. SIMMER, STIRRING CONSTANTLY UNTIL THICK, ABOUT 10 MINUTES. ADD BROWN SUGAR OR HONEY AND COMBINE. COOL AND STIR IN POWDERED MILK AND VANILLA. CHILL.

FOR A DELICIOUS CAROB DRINK, STIR 2 TO 3 TBSP. OF SYRUP INTO 8 OZ. OF HOT OR COLD MILK! THE SYRUP WILL KEEP SEVERAL WEEKS IN THE REFRIGERATOR.

SHAKE-A-MEAL SMOOTHIE

MAKES 3 TO 4 CUPS

A DELICIOUS, NUTRITIOUS DRINK!

```
1 1/2  CUPS MILK
1  TBSP. CAROB POWDER
3/4  CUP  POWDERED MILK
1/8  TSP. CINNAMON
1/2  TSP. VANILLA
4  TBSP.  PEANUT BUTTER
1  RIPE BANANA
HONEY  TO  TASTE
6  ICE CUBES
```

Ring the bell!

Knock at the door!

Lift up the latch!

And walk in!

COMBINE IN A BLENDER
JAR THE MILK, CAROB POWDER,
POWDERED MILK, CINNAMON,
VANILLA, AND PEANUT BUTTER.
BLEND FOR THIRTY SECONDS.
ADD THE BANANA, (CUT INTO
1 INCH CHUNKS) AND BLEND
30 SECONDS MORE.
TASTE FOR SWEETNESS BEFORE
ADDING ANY HONEY.
ADD ICE CUBES TWO AT A
TIME, AND BLEND UNTIL
THEY ARE DISSOLVED AND
SHAKE IS VERY THICK.
MAKES 3 LARGE OR 4
SMALL SERVINGS.

A QUICK FEAST!

SUNDAE SAUCE

MAKES 3 CUPS

    2   TBSP. BUTTER
    1/2 CUP MILK
    1   CUP HONEY
    1/3 CUP CAROB POWDER
    1/4 TSP. SALT
    1   CUP CHOPPED NUTS
             (OPTIONAL)
    1/2 TSP. VANILLA EXTRACT

MELT THE BUTTER.   ADD MILK, HONEY, AND CAROB POWDER.   COOK, STIRRING CONSTANTLY, UNTIL THE MIXTURE BOILS, THEN LOWER HEAT AND BOIL GENTLY FOR 5 MINUTES, STIRRING CONSTANTLY.   ADD SALT. REMOVE FROM HEAT AND BEAT SAUCE UNTIL IT IS SMOOTH AND CREAMY.   STIR IN NUTS. LET SAUCE COOL FIVE MINUTES, STIRRING OCCASIONALLY, THEN ADD VANILLA. SERVE THE SAUCE WARM OVER CAKE OR ICE CREAM.

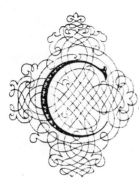 AROB SHAKE

MAKES 1 TO 2 SERVINGS

1 CUP MILK
1 TBSP. CAROB POWDER
1/2 CUP POWDERED MILK
1/8 TSP. CINNAMON
1/2 TSP. VANILLA
1 TO 2 TSP. HONEY (TO TASTE)
4 ICE CUBES

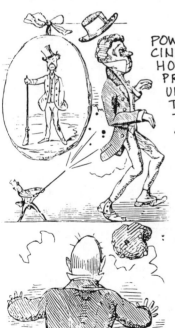

COMBINE MILK, CAROB POWDER, POWDERED MILK, CINNAMON, VANILLA, AND HONEY IN A BLENDER JAR. PROCESS FOR 30 SECONDS, UNTIL WELL MIXED. ADD THE ICE CUBES, ONE AT A TIME, AND BLEND UNTIL SHAKE IS THICK AND FROSTY. MAKES 1 HUGE OR 2 SMALL SERVINGS.

CREPE STACK

SERVES 6 TO 8

AND YET ANOTHER GREAT DESSERT!

4 OZ. CAROB CHIPS
1 TBSP. WATER
2 EGG YOLKS
HONEY OR MAPLE SYRUP TO TASTE
1 CUP HEAVY CREAM, WHIPPED
10 COOKED CAROB CREPES
   (RECIPE ON PAGE 25)
SLIVERED ALMONDS

PUT CAROB CHIPS AND WATER IN A DOUBLE BOILER OVER VERY HOT WATER AND STIR UNTIL CHIPS MELT. DO NOT LET THE WATER TOUCH THE TOP PART OF THE DOUBLE BOILER. ADD EGG YOLKS, ONE AT A TIME, BEATING WELL AFTER EACH ONE. IF YOU USE UNSWEETENED CAROB CHIPS, YOU MAY WANT TO ADD A LITTLE HONEY OR MAPLE SYRUP, BUT TASTE TO DECIDE. REMOVE CAROB MIXTURE FROM THE HEAT AND COOL. FOLD IN THE WHIPPED CREAM WHEN COMPLETELY COOLED.

SPREAD CAROB-CREAM MIXTURE EVENLY OVER EACH CREPE. STACK CREPES ON TOP OF EACH OTHER AND CHILL FOR SEVERAL HOURS. CUT INTO WEDGES AND SERVE GARNISHED WITH SLIVERED ALMONDS.

DESSERT CREPES

```
3   EGGS
1   CUP FLOUR
1 1/4 CUPS BUTTERMILK
2   TBSP. CAROB POWDER
1   TBSP. HONEY
2   TBSP. MELTED BUTTER OR
              MARGARINE
```

COMBINE ALL INGREDIENTS IN A BLENDER JAR AND PROCESS FOR ONE MINUTE. SCRAPE SIDES OF JAR WITH A SPATULA AND BLEND FOR 15 SECONDS MORE. REFRIGERATE BATTER AT LEAST 1 HOUR BEFORE COOKING CREPES. STIR BATTER GENTLY BEFORE MAKING EACH CREPE.

FOR A DELICIOUS DESSERT TRY THIS:

 "CAROB CREPE DESSERT"

SPOON 2 TBSP. OF TIA MARIA MOUSSE (RECIPE ON PAGE 44) DOWN THE CENTER OF EACH CREPE. ROLL UP AND PUT SEAM SIDE DOWN ON A SERVING PLATTER OR INDIVIDUAL PLATES. GARNISH EACH CREPE WITH A SPOONFUL OF WHIPPED CREAM AND A FEW CAROB CHIPS.

NOTES

QUICK BREADS, CAKES, & FROSTINGS

The merry musician groaned again,
His fiddle was in his hand
A tune he tried, "The last," he sighed,
"I ever shall play on land."

'Twas a polka gay, and, oh, strange to say,
When the Crocodile heard the sound,
He laughed and rose on the tip of his toes,
And began to caper round.

GINGER BREAD

MAKES 1 5"× 9" LOAF

A DELICIOUSLY DIFFERENT GINGERBREAD!

PRE-HEAT OVEN TO 350°

1 EGG
1/2 CUP MOLASSES
1/4 CUP HONEY
1/2 CUP OIL
1-1/2 CUPS WHOLE WHEAT
        FLOUR
1/4 CUP CAROB POWDER
1 TSP. BAKING POWDER
1/2 TSP. BAKING SODA
1/2 TSP. SALT
2 TSP. CINNAMON
1 TO 2 TSP. GROUND GINGER
1/2 CUP HOT WATER

MIX EGG, MOLASSES, HONEY, AND OIL. SIFT TOGETHER FLOUR, CAROB POWDER, BAKING POWDER, BAKING SODA, SALT, CINNAMON, AND GINGER. STIR GENTLY INTO MOLASSES MIXTURE ALONG WITH THE HOT WATER.

IMMEDIATELY POUR INTO A GREASED 5" X 9" LOAF PAN. BAKE AT 350° FOR 30 MINUTES, OR UNTIL BREAD SPRINGS BACK WHEN PRESSED COOL IN PAN 10 MINUTES BEFORE TURNING OUT.

GREAT SERVED WARM WITH WHIPPED CREAM!

DOUBLE FUDGE CAKE

1 8" SQUARE CAKE

A VERY RICH AND MOIST CAKE!

PRE-HEAT OVEN TO 350°

1 CUP WHOLE WHEAT FLOUR
1/3 CUP CAROB POWDER
1 TSP. INSTANT COFFEE
        (OPTIONAL)
1/2 TSP. BAKING SODA
1/2 TSP. BAKING POWDER
1/2 TSP. SALT
1/2 CUP BUTTER OR
             MARGARINE
1 CUP BROWN SUGAR
2 EGGS
1/2 CUP BUTTERMILK
1 TSP. VANILLA
1 CUP CAROB CHIPS
1/2 CUP CHOPPED NUTS

SIFT TOGETHER FLOUR, CAROB POWDER, INSTANT COFFEE, BAKING POWDER, BAKING SODA, AND SALT. SET ASIDE. CREAM BUTTER AND BROWN SUGAR. ADD EGGS AND BEAT UNTIL FLUFFY. ADD THE DRY MIXTURE ALTERNATELY WITH THE BUTTERMILK. STIR IN VANILLA, CAROB CHIPS, AND CHOPPED NUTS. POUR BATTER INTO A WELL GREASED 8 OR 9 INCH SQUARE PAN. BAKE AT 350° FOR 30 TO 35 MINUTES, OR UNTIL CENTER SPRINGS BACK WHEN PRESSED. COOL IN THE PAN ON A RACK.

SERVE PLAIN OR WITH A RICH THICK FROSTING.

29

APPLESAUCE CAKE

1 8" SQUARE CAKE

PRE-HEAT OVEN TO 350°

```
1/2   CUP  SOFT TOFU OR 1 EGG
1/3   CUP  CAROB CHIPS
1/3   CUP  SALAD OIL
1/4   CUP  BROWN SUGAR
1     TBSP. CAROB POWDER
1     CUP  APPLESAUCE
1/2   TSP. SALT
1/8   TSP. GROUND CLOVES
1/2   TSP. CINNAMON
1     TSP. VANILLA
2     TBSP. CORN STARCH
1-1/2 CUPS WHOLE WHEAT PASTRY FLOUR
1     TSP. BAKING SODA
1     TSP. CREAM OF TARTAR
3/4   CUP  CHOPPED NUTS
```
CREAMY CAROB FROSTING (SEE PAGE 40)

CONTINUED NEXT PAGE ...

APPLESAUCE CAKE, CONTINUED

COMBINE DRAINED TOFU, CAROB CHIPS, SALAD OIL, BROWN SUGAR, CAROB POWDER, APPLESAUCE, SALT, GROUND CLOVES CINNAMON, VANILLA, AND CORNSTARCH IN A FOOD PROCESSER OR BLENDER. PROCESS UNTIL CAROB CHIPS ARE BROKEN UP INTO SMALL PIECES.

SIFT FLOUR, BAKING SODA, AND CREAM OF TARTAR. ADD ALL AT ONCE AND MIX QUICKLY UNTIL JUST MOISTENED. STIR IN THE CHOPPED NUTS. NOTE: IF YOU HAVE USED A BLENDER TO COMBINE CAROB MIXTURE, POUR IT OUT OF THE BLENDER JAR AND INTO A MIXING BOWL BEFORE ADDING FLOUR MIXTURE AND CHOPPED NUTS.

SPOON BATTER INTO A WELL GREASED SMALL TUBE PAN OR 8 INCH SQUARE PAN. BAKE AT 350° FOR ABOUT 1 HOUR. THE CAKE IS DONE WHEN THE EDGES PULL AWAY FROM THE SIDES OF THE PAN. PLACE ON A RACK TO COOL. WHEN COOLED, FROST WITH CREAMY CAROB FROSTING AND SAY IT ALL CAME FROM THE HOUSE THAT JACK BUILT!

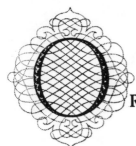

ORANGE CAROB CHIP CAKE

MAKES 1 7"×11" CAKE

A MOIST FLAVORFUL CAKE!

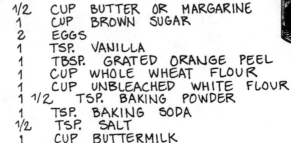

PRE~HEAT OVEN TO 350°

1/2 CUP BUTTER OR MARGARINE
1 CUP BROWN SUGAR
2 EGGS
1 TSP. VANILLA
1 TBSP. GRATED ORANGE PEEL
1 CUP WHOLE WHEAT FLOUR
1 CUP UNBLEACHED WHITE FLOUR
1 1/2 TSP. BAKING POWDER
1 TSP. BAKING SODA
1/2 TSP. SALT
1 CUP BUTTERMILK
1 1/2 CUPS CAROB CHIPS
1/2 CUP CHOPPED WALNUTS

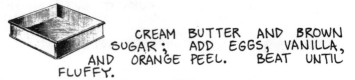

CREAM BUTTER AND BROWN SUGAR; ADD EGGS, VANILLA, AND ORANGE PEEL. BEAT UNTIL FLUFFY.

IN A SEPARATE BOWL, MIX TOGETHER FLOURS, BAKING POWDER, BAKING SODA, AND SALT. ADD TO BUTTER MIXTURE ALTERNATELY WITH THE BUTTERMILK, MIXING WELL AFTER EACH ADDITION. STIR IN 1 CUP OF CAROB CHIPS. POUR BATTER INTO A WELL GREASED 7" × 11" BAKING PAN. COMBINE REMAINING 1/2 CUP CAROB CHIPS AND CHOPPED NUTS AND SPRINKLE OVER THE TOP. PRESS THEM IN LIGHTLY.

BAKE AT 350° FOR 45 MINUTES, OR UNTIL CENTER SPRINGS BACK WHEN TOUCHED. COOL IN PAN ON A RACK. SERVE WARM OR COLD.

PERSIMMON BREAD

MAKES 1 LOAF

PRE-HEAT OVEN TO 400°

1/2   CUP PERSIMMON PULP *
1/4   CUP TOFU OR 1 EGG
1/2   CUP MARGARINE OR OIL
1/2   CUP BUTTERMILK
1   TSP. VANILLA
2 TO 4 TBSP. HONEY
1 1/4 CUPS WHOLE WHEAT FLOUR
1/4   CUP CAROB POWDER
2   TSP. BAKING POWDER
1/2   TSP. BAKING SODA
1/2   TSP. SALT
2   TSP. PUMPKIN PIE
              SPICE
1/2 TO 2/3 CUP RAISINS

COMBINE THE PERSIMMON, TOFU,
MARGARINE, BUTTERMILK, VANILLA,
AND HONEY IN A FOOD PROCESSOR OR
BLENDER AND BEAT UNTIL SMOOTH. COMBINE THE
DRY INGREDIENTS AND RAISINS IN A MIXING BOWL
AND STIR WELL. ADD THE PERSIMMON MIXTURE
AND MIX ONLY UNTIL THE DRY INGREDIENTS ARE
MOISTENED. SPOON INTO A GREASED 5" x 9"
LOAF PAN AND BAKE AT 400° FOR ABOUT 40
MINUTES OR UNTIL THE CENTER SPRINGS BACK
WHEN PRESSED. REMOVE TO A RACK AND COOL
FOR ABOUT 10 MINUTES. TURN OUT AND ALLOW
              THE BREAD TO COOL COMPLETELY
              BEFORE SLICING.

              THIS RECIPE CAN
           BE MADE WITH ANY KIND
           OF FRESH OR COOKED
FRUIT PUREE SUCH AS
APPLESAUCE, CRANBERRY
SAUCE OR PUMPKIN.

BANANA SEED BREAD

MAKES 1 LOAF

PRE-HEAT OVEN TO 350°

2 SMALL RIPE BANANAS
1/4 CUP SOFT TOFU <u>OR</u>
1 EGG
1/3 CUP OIL
1/4 CUP HONEY
1/4 CUP BUTTERMILK
1 TSP. VANILLA
1 1/4 CUPS WHOLE WHEAT FLOUR
1/4 CUP CAROB POWDER
1/4 CUP WHEAT GERM OR BRAN
2 TSP. BAKING POWDER
1/2 TSP. BAKING SODA
1/4 TSP. SALT
2 TBSP. POPPY SEEDS
2 TBSP. MILLET OR
SESAME SEEDS

MASH THE BANANAS WITH TOFU AND MIX WELL. THIS CAN BE DONE IN A FOOD PROCESSOR OR MIXER. ADD THE OIL, HONEY, VANILLA, AND BUTTERMILK AND BEAT UNTIL SMOOTH. MIX ALL DRY INGREDIENTS TOGETHER IN A LARGE BOWL. ADD THE WET MIXTURE AND STIR ONLY ENOUGH TO MIX WELL, DO NOT BEAT. THE BATTER WILL BE QUITE THICK. SPOON INTO A 5" x 9" LOAF PAN AND BAKE IN A 350° OVEN FOR ABOUT 40 MINUTES, OR UNTIL THE CENTER SPRINGS BACK WHEN PRESSED. LET THE BREAD STAND ON A RACK FOR 10 MINUTES AND AND THEN TURN OUT TO COOL.

CAROB CUPCAKES

MAKES 30 TO 36

PRE-HEAT OVEN TO 325°

```
3    CUPS  WHOLE  WHEAT  FLOUR
1/2  CUP   CAROB  POWDER
1    TSP.  SALT
1    TSP.  CINNAMON
3    TSP.  BAKING  SODA
1    CUP   BUTTER  OR  MARGARINE
3/4  CUP   BROWN  SUGAR
2    EGGS
1    TSP.  VANILLA
2    CUPS  SOUR  CREAM  OR  YOGURT
```

SIFT TOGETHER THE FLOUR, CAROB POWDER, SALT, CINNAMON, AND BAKING SODA. CREAM TOGETHER THE BUTTER AND BROWN SUGAR. ADD EGGS AND VANILLA AND BEAT UNTIL FLUFFY. ADD FLOUR MIXTURE AND SOUR CREAM ALTERNATELY, BEATING CAREFULLY AFTER EACH ADDITION. GREASE MUFFIN TINS, OR LINE WITH PAPER BAKING CUPS. FILL EACH NO MORE THAN 3/4 FULL. BAKE FOR 25 MINUTES, OR UNTIL CUPCAKES SPRING BACK WHEN TOUCHED. COOL AND FROST IF DESIRED.

BRAN-APPLE MUFFINS

MAKES 15 TO 18

PRE-HEAT OVEN TO 375°

1 CUP WHOLE WHEAT FLOUR
1 CUP BRAN
3 TSP. BAKING POWDER
1/2 TSP. SALT
1/2 TSP. CINNAMON
2 TBSP. CAROB POWDER
4 TBSP. HONEY
1 EGG
1/2 CUP MILK
1 CUP APPLESAUCE
1/4 CUP OIL

SIFT TOGETHER FLOUR, BAKING POWDER, SALT, CINNAMON, AND CAROB POWDER. STIR IN THE BRAN. IN A SMALL BOWL, MIX THE HONEY, EGG, MILK, APPLESAUCE, AND OIL. ADD THE WET MIXTURE ALL AT ONCE TO THE DRY INGREDIENTS, STIRRING ONLY UNTIL FLOUR MIXTURE IS MOISTENED. FILL OILED MUFFIN TINS (OR USE PAPER LINERS) TWO-THIRDS FULL. BAKE AT 375° FOR 20 MINUTES.

A GREAT MUFFIN !

SPICE CAKE

1 8" OR 9" SQUARE
CAKE

PRE-HEAT OVEN TO 350°

1 1/2 CUPS WHOLE WHEAT
PASTRY FLOUR
1/3 CUP CAROB POWDER
1/2 TSP. BAKING POWDER
1/2 TSP. BAKING SODA
1/2 TSP. SALT
1 1/2 TSP. CINNAMON
1/2 TSP. ALLSPICE
1/4 TSP. GROUND CLOVES
1/2 CUP BUTTER OR
MARGARINE
1 CUP BROWN SUGAR
1/2 CUP BUTTERMILK
1 TSP. VANILLA
3/4 CUP CHOPPED WALNUTS

SIFT TOGETHER FLOUR, CAROB POWDER,
BAKING POWDER, BAKING SODA, SALT,
CINNAMON, ALLSPICE, AND CLOVES.
SET ASIDE. CREAM THE
BUTTER AND BROWN SUGAR;
ADD EGGS AND BEAT UNTIL
FLUFFY. ADD FLOUR
MIXTURE ALTERNATELY WITH
THE BUTTERMILK AND
VANILLA. STIR IN CHOPPED
NUTS. POUR INTO A
WELL GREASED 8 OR 9
INCH SQUARE PAN AND
BAKE AT 350° FOR 30 TO
35 MINUTES, OR UNTIL
CAKE CENTER SPRINGS
BACK WHEN PRESSED.
COOL IN PAN ON RACK
AND FROST WITH HONEY
FROSTING.

BUTTERCREAM FROSTING

MAKES ABOUT 1/2 CUP

1/4 CUP BUTTER, SOFTENED
1 EGG
1/4 CUP CAROB POWDER, SIFTED
1/2 TSP. INSTANT COFFEE
1/2 TSP. VANILLA
DASH OF SALT
1 1/2 CUPS SIFTED POWDERED
      SUGAR
2 TBSP. HEAVY CREAM

BEAT BUTTER, EGG, AND CAROB POWDER UNTIL SMOOTH. ADD INSTANT COFFEE, VANILLA, AND SALT. BEAT IN POWDERED SUGAR UNTIL THICK. SLOWLY ADD THE CREAM, BEATING UNTIL FROSTING IS SMOOTH AND CREAMY.

ONEY FROSTING

MAKES 1 1/4 CUPS

1/4 CUP BUTTER OR
      MARGARINE
1/4 CUP HONEY
3/4 CUP NON-INSTANT
      POWDERED MILK
1/4 CUP CAROB POWDER
1 TSP. VANILLA
PINCH OF CINNAMON
PINCH OF NUTMEG
MILK OR LIGHT CREAM

CREAM THE BUTTER AND HONEY UNTIL SMOOTH. SIFT TOGETHER THE NON-INSTANT POWDERED MILK (THE INSTANT KIND WILL NOT WORK) AND THE CAROB POWDER. ADD TO THE BUTTER-HONEY MIXTURE AND BLEND UNTIL SMOOTH. STIR IN THE VANILLA AND SPICES. ADD THE MILK OR CREAM DROP BY DROP UNTIL FROSTING IS A LITTLE SOFTER THAN DESIRED. IT WILL FIRM UP AFTER IT IS SREAD ON YOUR CAKE OR CUPCAKES.

CREAMY FROSTING

MAKES ABOUT 1-1/4 CUPS

```
1/4  CUP  CAROB  POWDER  (SIFTED)
8    OZ.  SOFT  CREAM  CHEESE
          OR  RICOTTA
1/2  TSP.  INSTANT  COFFEE
1/4  CUP  MAPLE  SYRUP  OR  HONEY
1/2  TSP.  VANILLA
```

BEAT THE CAROB POWDER, CREAM CHEESE, AND INSTANT COFFEE TOGETHER. STIR IN THE MAPLE SYRUP OR HONEY, AND VANILLA. CHILL FOR AN HOUR BEFORE USING TO MAKE THE FROSTING FIRM.

40

NOTES

PUDDING, PIES,
& PANCAKES

The merry musician played and played,
    And faster his fingers flew;
While close to the Nile the Crocodile
    Danced faster and faster too.
At length he stopped, and down he dropped,
    Too giddy to hear or see;
And when he came round, his prey he found
    Had run away home to tea!

H.R.MILLAR

TIA MARIA MOUSSE

SERVES 4

```
1 TBSP.  GELATIN (1 ENVELOPE)
1/3 CUP  COLD  WATER
1  CUP   MILK
1/4 CUP  HONEY
1/2 CUP  CAROB CHIPS
2  TBSP.  BUTTER OR MARGARINE
1  CUP   SOFT TOFU
2  TSP.   VANILLA
1/4 CUP  TIA MARIA OR OTHER LIQUID *
2  EGG   WHITES
```

SOFTEN THE GELATIN IN THE COLD WATER AND SET ASIDE. COMBINE THE MILK, HONEY, CAROB CHIPS, AND BUTTER IN A SAUCEPAN AND HEAT, STIRRING CONSTANTLY, UNTIL CAROB MELTS. REMOVE FROM HEAT AND ADD THE GELATIN, MIXING UNTIL THE GELATIN MELTS. COMBINE THIS MIXTURE WITH THE TOFU, VANILLA, AND THE LIQUEUR OR JUICE, IN A BLENDER OR FOOD PROCESSOR AND BEAT UNTIL VERY SMOOTH. POUR INTO A MIXING BOWL AND REFRIGERATE.

REMOVE FROM REFRIGERATOR WHEN SET. FIRST BEAT THE EGG WHITES UNTIL VERY STIFF. THEN BEAT THE MOUSSE MIXTURE UNTIL FOAMY. FOLD THE EGG WHITES INTO THE MOUSSE. FILL INDIVIDUAL SERVING DISHES ~ WINE GLASSES DO VERY NICELY ~ AND REFRIGERATE FOR AT LEAST ONE HOUR BEFORE SERVING. GARNISH WITH CHOPPED NUTS AND A DAB OF JAM.

* YOU CAN USE CURACAO, AMARETTO, BRANDY, OR FRUIT JUICE SUCH AS APPLE, OR ORANGE JUICE + 1/2 TSP. GRATED ORANGE RIND.

BROWN RICE PUDDING

MAKES 4 TO 6 SERVINGS

PRE-HEAT OVEN TO 300°

1/4	CUP BROWN RICE
1	EGG
2	CUPS MILK OR SOYMILK
1/4	CUP HONEY
1	TABLESPOON BUTTER
1/3	CUP CAROB CHIPS

WASH THE RICE. BEAT THE EGG SLIGHTLY AND COMBINE WITH MILK, HONEY, AND RICE IN A GREASED ONE QUART CASSEROLE. COVER THE DISH AND PLACE IN A 300° OVEN FOR AN HOUR OR MORE, IF THICK PUDDING IS DESIRABLE. REMOVE FROM OVEN AND TASTE TO BE SURE THE RICE IS FULLY COOKED, AND THEN ADD THE BUTTER. FOLD IN THE CAROB CHIPS. SERVE WARM OR COLD.

TOFU CAROB PUDDING

SERVES 4 TO 6

16 OZ. SOFT TOFU
1/3 CUP CAROB POWDER
1/4 CUP HONEY
1/3 CUP PEANUT BUTTER
1/2 TSP. VANILLA
1/4 TO 1/2 CUP MILK OR
SOYMILK

DRAIN WATER FROM THE TOFU AND MASH IT SLIGHTLY WITH A FORK. IN A BLENDER OR FOOD PROCESSOR COMBINE THE TOFU, CAROB POWDER, HONEY, PEANUT BUTTER, AND VANILLA. BLEND UNTIL SMOOTH, ADDING MILK A LITTLE AT A TIME TO HELP MAKE BLENDING EASIER. WHEN PUDDING IS WELL MIXED AND SMOOTH, SPOON IT INTO SMALL BOWLS AND CHILL UNTIL SERVING TIME.

EASY AS ONE, TOFU, THREE... AND GREAT!

HASTY CAROB PUDDING

MAKES 4 TO 6 PORTIONS

1/2	CUP	BROWN SUGAR
1/2	CUP	BISCUIT MIX
1/2	CUP	CAROB POWDER
2	CUPS	MILK
1	CUP	WATER
1	TBSP.	BUTTER OR MARGARINE

MIX BROWN SUGAR, BISCUIT MIX, AND CAROB POWDER IN A 3 QUART SAUCEPAN. GRADUALLY WHISK IN THE MILK AND THE WATER. COOK OVER MEDIUM HIGH HEAT UNTIL MIXTURE THICKENS AND COMES TO A SLOW BOIL. LOWER HEAT AND SIMMER, STIRRING OFTEN, FOR 5 MINUTES. REMOVE FROM HEAT AND ADD BUTTER. COOL, STIRRING OCCASIONALLY. POUR INTO A BOWL AND CHILL.

VERY FESTIVE WHEN SERVED IN TALL WINE GLASSES AND TOPPED WITH WHIPPED CREAM.

JONNY-CAROB CAKES

THE CAROB MAKES TRADITIONAL
PANCAKES NATURALLY SWEET.
THEY CAN BE SERVED WITH JUST
A DAB OF JAM.

1 CUP CORN MEAL
1/4 CUP CAROB POWDER
1/2 TSP. SALT (TO TASTE)
1 1/2 CUPS BOILING WATER
1/3 CUP THICK CREAM, YOGURT,
        SOFT TOFU, OR
        SOUR CREAM
OIL FOR FRYING

MIX THE CORNMEAL, SALT, AND CAROB
IN A MIXING BOWL. SLOWLY ADD THE BOILING
WATER AND BEAT FOR 3 OR 4 MINUTES, UNTIL
THE MIXTURE IS A LITTLE THICKER THAN
PANCAKE BATTER. STIR IN THE CREAM (OR
YOUR OWN CHOICE).

GREASE A GRIDDLE AND PLACE OVER
        MEDIUM HEAT. DROP CAKES BY
        SPOONFULS, QUITE FAR APART
        TO LEAVE ROOM TO EXPAND.
        BROWN WELL ON BOTH SIDES.
        SERVE WITH BUTTER,
        OR BETTER YET, AS
        AN UNUSUAL
        DESSERT ~ HOT
        WITH ICE
        CREAM!

CAROB PIE CRUST

1 1/3 CUPS UNBLEACHED OR WHOLE WHEAT PASTRY FLOUR
3   TBSP. CAROB POWDER
1/2 TSP. BAKING POWDER
1/2 TSP. SALT (OPTIONAL)
1/8 TSP. CINNAMON
1/3 CUP   SHORTENING
1/4 CUP   ICE WATER (MORE OR LESS)

COMBINE THE DRY INGREDIENTS AND MIX WELL. CUT IN THE SHORTENING UNTIL MIXTURE IS MEAL-LIKE. ADD THE ICE WATER, GRADUALLY, AND MIX UNTIL DOUGH LEAVES THE SIDES OF THE BOWL. USE MORE WATER, IF NEEDED, BUT ADD IT BY DROPS. TOO MUCH WATER MAKES A TOUGH CRUST. ROLL OUT BETWEEN TWO SHEETS OF WAXED PAPER FOR A BOTTOM CRUST FOR AN 8 INCH TO 10 INCH PIE. FOR A DOUBLE CRUST, DOUBLE THE RECIPE.

FOR A "PRE-COOKED" PIE SHELL, HEAT OVEN TO 350°. LINE THE PIE PAN WITH DOUGH AND PIERCE ALL OVER THE BOTTOM AND SIDES WITH A FORK. BAKE FOR 10 TO 15 MINUTES. COOL ON A RACK. PIE CRUST IS NOW READY FOR YOUR FAVORITE PIE FILLING.

 SILKEN PIE

1 TBSP. UNFLAVORED GELATIN
3/4 CUP COLD WATER
1 CUP MILK
1 CUP CAROB CHIPS
1/4 TSP. SALT (OPTIONAL)
1/3 CUP HONEY
1 TBSP. BUTTER
3 EGG YOLKS
2 TSP. VANILLA
1/2 TSP. ALMOND EXTRACT
1 TBSP. MALT POWDER OR
   1 TSP. INSTANT COFFEE
3 EGG WHITES
1/2 CUP WHIPPING CREAM

1 PRE~BAKED PIE CRUST

SOFTEN THE GELATIN IN THE WATER, SET ASIDE. COMBINE THE MILK, CAROB CHIPS, SALT, AND HONEY IN A HEAVY BOTTOM SAUCEPAN AND BRING TO A BOIL, STIRRING CONSTANTLY. REMOVE FROM HEAT AND ADD THE EGG YOLKS, ONE AT A TIME, BEATING WELL AFTER EACH ADDITION. RETURN TO MEDIUM HEAT AND BRING JUST TO A SIMMER, STIRRING UNTIL THE MIXTURE THICKENS.
DO NOT BOIL!

REMOVE FROM THE HEAT AGAIN, AND ADD THE GELATIN MIXTURE AND THE BUTTER, STIRRING UNTIL THEY ARE COMPLETELY MELTED.

CONTINUED NEXT PAGE...

SILKEN PIE, CONTINUED

MIX IN THE FLAVORINGS AND STRAIN INTO A BOWL; THIS WILL REMOVE ANY LUMPS WHICH ARE NOT VERY DESIRABLE IN A SILK PIE. REFRIGERATE UNTIL SET.

WHEN THE MIXTURE IS SET, BEGIN TO ASSEMBLE THE PIE. BEAT THE EGGWHITES UNTIL STIFF. BEAT THE WHIPPING CREAM. THEN BEAT THE CAROB MIXTURE UNTIL IT IS LIGHT. CAREFULLY FOLD THE WHIPPED CREAM AND BEATEN EGGWHITES INTO THE CAROB MIXTURE. SPOON THIS INTO THE PREPARED AND COMPLETELY COOLED CRUST AND REFRIGERATE FOR SEVERAL HOURS BEFORE SERVING.

THIS CAN ALSO BE SERVED AS A DELICATE MOUSSE. FILL TALL STEM GLASSES OR A BEAUTIFUL GLASS BOWL AND GARNISH WITH A BERRY OR CHERRY OR A DAB OF RASPBERRY JAM. THIS IS A SUPERLATIVE WHEN SERVED WITH A RASPBERRY SAUCE.

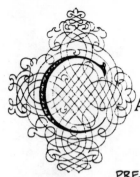

CAROB PECAN PIE

MAKES 1 9" PIE

PRE-HEAT OVEN TO 375°

1 CAROB PIE CRUST (PAGE 49)
1 CUP CAROB CHIPS (UNSWEETENED)
1/4 CUP BUTTER OR MARGARINE
1-1/3 CUP MILK
1/2 CUP POWDERED MILK
3/4 CUP HONEY
2 EGGS
3 TBSP. UNBLEACHED WHITE
        FLOUR
1/8 TSP. SALT
1 TSP. VANILLA
1 CUP PECAN NUTS

MIX CAROB PIE CRUST. ROLL OUT AND LINE A 9 INCH PIE PAN. FLUTE THE EDGE AND REFRIGERATE UNTIL FILLING IS PREPARED.

COMBINE CAROB CHIPS, BUTTER, MILK, AND POWDERED MILK IN A MEDIUM SAUCEPAN. COOK OVER LOW HEAT STIRRING CONSTANTLY WITH A WIRE WHISK UNTIL CAROB CHIPS ARE MELTED AND MIXTURE IS SMOOTH. STIR IN THE HONEY AND REMOVE FROM HEAT. PUT EGGS, FLOUR, SALT, AND VANILLA IN A BLENDER JAR AND BLEND UNTIL VERY SMOOTH. WITH BLENDER ON LOW SPEED, SLOWLY POUR IN THE CAROB CHIP MIXTURE. WHEN THOROUGHLY MIXED, POUR INTO PREPARED PIE SHELL. SPRINKLE PECANS EVENLY OVER TOP OF PIE. BAKE AT 375° FOR 45 MINUTES, OR UNTIL PIE IS FIRM IN THE CENTER. COOL COMPLETELY BEFORE SERVING.

PUMPKIN-CAROB CHEESE PIE

MAKES 1 9" PIE

PRE-HEAT OVEN TO 425°

1 UNBAKED PIE CRUST

2 OZ. CHEDDAR CHEESE
2 EGGS, SEPARATED
1 CUP SOFT TOFU
1/2 CUP CAROB POWDER
1/2 CUP OIL
2/3 CUP BUTTERMILK
1/3 CUP HONEY OR UNREFINED SUGAR
1/4 CUP UNBLEACHED WHITE FLOUR
1/4 TSP. SALT
1 TSP. VANILLA
2/3 CUP COOKED PUMPKIN
2 TSP. LEMON JUICE
1/2 TSP. PUMPKIN PIE SPICE

CUT CHEESE IN SMALL CHUNKS AND COMBINE WITH EGG YOLKS, TOFU, CAROB POWDER, OIL AND BUTTERMILK IN A FOOD PROCESSOR OR BLENDER. BLEND UNTIL VERY SMOOTH. ADD THE REST OF THE INGREDIENTS AND BLEND AGAIN UNTIL VERY SMOOTH. BEAT THE EGG WHITES UNTIL STIFF; THEN FOLD THE PUMPKIN MIXTURE AND BEATEN EGG WHITES TOGETHER. POUR INTO UNBAKED PIE SHELL. PLACE IN 425° OVEN AND REDUCE HEAT TO 350° IMMEDIATELY. BAKE FOR ABOUT 45 MINUTES, OR UNTIL A KNIFE INSERTED IN THE CENTER COMES OUT CLEAN. COOL ON A RACK AND SERVE WARM OR CHILL IN THE REFRIGERATOR AND SERVE COLD. DELIGHTFUL!

COCONUT CREAM PIE

MAKES 1 9" PIE

PREPARE AND PRE-BAKE A CAROB
CRUST PIE SHELL (PAGE 49)

3 TBSP. CORNSTARCH OR
   2 TBSP. ARROWROOT
2 1/2 CUPS MILK OR SOYMILK
1/4 CUP HONEY, OR TO TASTE
2 EGGS (OPTIONAL)
2 TSP. BUTTER (OPTIONAL)
1 TSP. VANILLA
1/2 CUP CAROB CHIPS
1/2 TO 3/4 CUP TOASTED, UNSWEETENED
         COCONUT

HAVE THE PIE SHELL READY AND COOLING
WHILE PUDDING IS PREPARED. MIX THE CORNSTARCH,
WITH 1/2 CUP COLD MILK; COMBINE WITH REMAINDER
OF MILK AND WITH HONEY IN A HEAVY-BOTTOMED
SAUCEPAN AND BRING TO A BOIL OVER MEDIUM
HEAT, STIRRING CONSTANTLY. BEAT THE EGGS
AND ADD ABOUT 1/2 CUP OF THE HOT CUSTARD
MIXTURE TO THEM, VERY GRADUALLY, WHILE
CONTINUING TO BEAT. ADD THE EGG MIXTURE TO
THE HOT CUSTARD, BEATING ALL
THE WHILE. BRING TO JUST
UNDER A BOIL; REMOVE FROM
HEAT AND ADD THE BUTTER.
COOL SLIGHTLY, AND MIX IN
THE VANILLA. POUR IN THE
CAROB CHIPS, STIRRING
SLOWLY SO THAT THE CHIPS
WILL MELT PARTIALLY TO
MAKE A SWIRL PATTERN IN
THE STILL HOT CUSTARD.
COOL COMPLETELY BEFORE
FILLING THE CRUST. SPRINKLE
THE COCONUT LIBERALLY OVER
THE TOP. CHILL BEFORE
SERVING.

54

NDEX

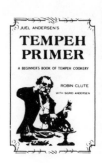